# A Note to Parent

*Eyewitness Readers* is a compelling new reading programme for children. *Eyewitness* has become the most trusted name in illustrated books and this new series combines the highly visual *Eyewitness* approach with engaging, easy-to-read stories. Each *Eyewitness Reader* is guaranteed to capture a child's interest while developing his or her reading skills, general knowledge and love of reading.

The books are written by leading children's authors and are designed in conjunction with literacy experts, including Cliff Moon M.Ed., Honorary Fellow of the University of Reading. Cliff Moon spent many years as a teacher and teacher educator specializing in reading. He has written more than 140 books for children and teachers, and he reviews regularly for teachers' journals.

The four levels of *Eyewitness Readers* are aimed at different reading abilities, enabling you to choose the books that are exactly right for each child.

**Level 1** – Beginning to read
**Level 2** – Beginning to read alone
**Level 3** – Reading alone
**Level 4** – Proficient readers

The "normal" age at which a child begins to read can be anywhere from three to eight years old, so these levels are intended only as a general guideline.

No matter which level you select, you can be sure that you're helping children learn to read, then read to learn!

www.dk.com

**Editor** Caroline Bingham
**Art Editor** Helen Melville

**Senior Editor** Linda Esposito
**Senior Art Editor** Diane Thistlethwaite
**Cover Designer** Giles Powell-Smith
**Production** Melanie Dowland
**Picture Researcher** Andrea Sadler
**Illustrator** Peter Dennis

**Reading Consultant**
Cliff Moon, M.Ed.

Published in Great Britain by
Dorling Kindersley Limited
9 Henrietta Street
London WC2E 8PS

2 4 6 8 10 9 7 5 3 1

Eyewitness Readers™ is a trademark of
Dorling Kindersley Limited, London.

A CIP catalogue record for this book is
available from the British Library.

ISBN 0-7513-6265-4

Colour reproduction by Colourscan, Singapore
Printed and bound in Belgium by Proost

The publisher would like to thank the following for
their kind permission to reproduce their photographs:
Key: a=above; c=centre; b=below; l=left; r=right; t=top

Allsport: Pascal Rondeau: front jacket b, 27br;
Corbis UK Ltd: 34cl; Frank Spooner Pictures: Art Seitz 24tl;
Liaison 20b; Poulet.Ph/Mission 20clb; NASA: front jacket cra,
36-37 b, 40-41, 40cl, 42-43b, 42clb, 43tr, 46bl;
National Motor Museum, Beaulieu: 18tl; Neill Bruce Motoring
Photolibrary: Peter Roberts Collection 44b;
Pictures Colour Library: 17cr, 39cr; Quadrant Picture Library:
25tr, 26tl, 32-33c, Rex Features: Anthony Upton 18-19b;
Pinson 21cr; The Times: 24-25 b; Science Photo Library:
NASA 42t; Sporting Pictures (U.K.) Ltd: 9cr;
Telegraph Colour Library: Planet Earth/Norbert Wu 20tl;
TRH Pictures: front jacket t, 32tl, 37tr, 46t, E. Nevill 47br.

# Contents

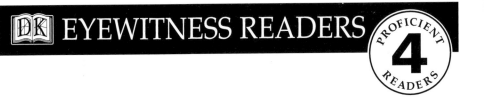

# EXTREME MACHINES

Written by Christopher Maynard

London • New York • Sydney • Delhi

**On land**
*Endeavor* holds the world's land speed record for the fastest truck. In 1993 it zipped along at a staggering 363 kph.

# An extreme machine

Most of the cars, boats and planes we travel in these days are reliable and safe. Most of them are perhaps a little ordinary too, because we see them every day. But there are lots of odd-looking machines that only exist to do something fantastic. They go ridiculously fast or fly incredibly high.

J621
110428

**On the sea**
Offshore powerboats race along more than three times faster than a car is allowed to travel on the motorway.

4

They are extreme machines. Most people would love to have a chance to see them close up or – even better – ride in them.

In this book you'll find out what some of the weirdest machines on Earth can do. You'll also find out how they work and how people risk their lives trying to take them to extremes.

**In the air**
The space shuttle is built to make many trips into space. Its cargo bay is so big it could hide a small whale.

**Ray power**
Solar cars are powered by the Sun's rays, not by petrol or diesel. This car, the *Mad Dog*, can reach more than 70 kph (but not on cloudy days!).

# Drag car racing

The two drivers sat in their
drag cars waiting for the next
400-metre race. They watched
an assistant splash water over both
sets of rear tyres, or slicks. The fat
slicks were now slippery as the
drivers locked their front brakes and
revved their gleaming engines.
With a roar that set the packed
stadium cheering, the slicks began
to spin. Clouds of smoke rose behind
the drag cars.

In seconds the rubber slicks turned soft with heat. It gave them a grip on the track that was as sticky as a leech's. There would be no unwanted wheel spin and wasted seconds when the race began, no matter how fast the drivers set off.

Each driver now popped his gear stick into first and gripped the handbrake to hold his car back. Each man felt the engines begin to tug. Before them was a "Christmas tree" of lights, stacked one above another on a pole. The cars were ready to spring forwards the instant the lights changed.

**Slow car?**
A Ferrari can reach 100 kph in about five seconds. Drag racers do it in just two!

**Safety first**
A drag car driver wears a fire-proof suit, a crash helmet and a neck brace to help prevent injury.

One of the Christmas tree's lights winked on, then another. A third flashed green and the two cars rocketed forwards. Blink and you would miss the race! Less than eight seconds later the cars screamed past the finish line 400 metres down the track. Having reached 240 kph, they were travelling well over twice as fast as a car on a motorway.

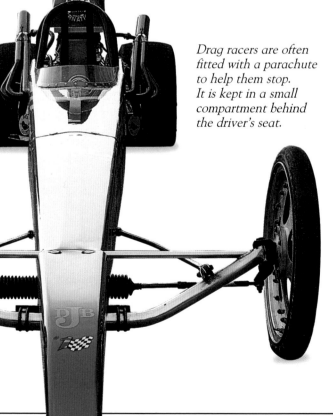

*Drag racers are often fitted with a parachute to help them stop. It is kept in a small compartment behind the driver's seat.*

The drivers released parachutes to help slow the cars. The race was so close that it was hard for the excited crowd to see which car had come first. Fortunately, the electronic timer caught it all. The winner, in the left-hand lane, was seven-hundredths of a second faster!

The drivers steered over to the road that led the loser from the racing lanes and the winner to his next race. Both drivers were handed a small ticket that noted the time of their run and their final speed.

For the rest of the day, the winning car beat every competitor it met. After two hours, the driver had won seven races. He had been racing for less than a minute in all.

**Not so quick**
Drag bikes are slower than drag cars. They have to be to avoid rearing up and doing wheelies. That would slow them down even more!

**Slower still**
Drag trucks are even slower than drag bikes. Because of their size, they take twice as long as a drag car to tear down a 400-metre strip.

**Getting dizzy**
Le Mans cars follow a circuit that is about 12 km long. They'll lap the circuit some 350 times during the race.

**Running start**
Drivers used to start Le Mans by running across the track and jumping into their cars. This no longer happens as it is very dangerous.

# Le Mans

One of the world's most famous endurance races is held every year close to Le Mans, a town in France.

The town comes alive each May and June when dozens of powerful cars and thousands of excited spectators arrive. The cars have come to take part in a gruelling 24-hour race round a long circuit near the town. It's fast, it's tiring, and it's thrilling!

In fact, although they only drive round a 12-km circuit, by the end of Le Mans the cars have covered almost 4,800 km. It's the same as crossing America once – and then coming more than a third of the way back!

On the day of the race, 70 to 80 cars pull away from the starting line. It's an incredible sight. Round and round the cars roar, circling the course in the time it takes to soft-boil an egg. Each car has a team of three drivers who change places after 15 circuits. That's just over an hour of driving each time.

The drivers need to stay as fresh as possible. If they get tired, it's easy to crash. That's why all Le Mans cars must have a towing eye on the front and back. The eye is used to tow them off the track if they crash.

**Wet or dry?**
Grooved tyres are used if it rains, smooth slicks if it's dry.

**Used once**
Windscreens usually last one race only: they are badly damaged in the 24 hours.

**Low = fast**
Le Mans cars are low, at just over one metre high, and wide. This helps them to hug the track, even at high speeds.

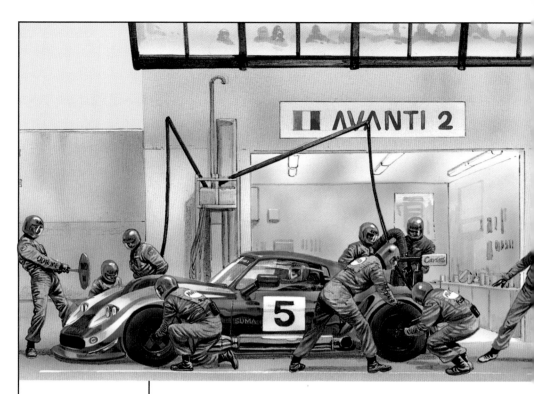

**Quick change**
A Le Mans car can be jacked up in seconds, raising the car 15 cm. Each wheel is held on with just one nut. Tyres are changed in the time it takes to tie a shoelace.

**Who's that?**
Racing machines always have numbers so they can be easily identified.

The best place to watch Le Mans is from the grandstands close to the pits – the areas where the cars are serviced. Cars regularly limp into the pits, thirsty for fuel, and urgently needing a new set of tyres.

Mechanics swarm round a car like bees the moment it rolls to a stop. Each mechanic has a small task that has been repeatedly rehearsed. Within seconds the car is refuelled, fitted with fresh tyres and speeding away.

AVANTI 3

**Tough truck**
This truck competed in an endurance race called the Baja 1000. This race covers 1,000 km in Mexico, over rocky and sandy ground.

The pits are busy, not only with cars, resting drivers and mechanics, but also with photographers and reporters. Behind the pits, each team has a huge garage with mountains of spare parts for the cars.

Drivers have to be careful when they leave the pits. Cold tyres don't grip as well as hot, and the cars may skid if they pull away too fast. It's a tricky race. That's why, in 1998, of the 73 cars that left the starting line only 23 managed to finish.

**Engine power**
Le Mans cars are fitted with engines that have four times the muscle of ordinary cars! Most engines are positioned behind the driver – not in front as in a family car.

# *Thrust SSC*

*Thrust SSC* (the initials stand for SuperSonic Car) was built to take the world land speed record. It was also the first car to go supersonic, or faster than the speed of sound – sound travels at about 1,224 kph. But the team of people who built the car almost didn't make an attempt at the speed record.

The car was built in Britain but it needed a long, flat stretch of ground to attempt a speed trial. Nowhere in Britain was suitable.

However, Black Rock Desert in Nevada, USA, was ideal. The desert is long and its surface is smooth. The problem was that the team couldn't afford to buy fuel for the aeroplane they needed to fly the car over.

Then someone suggested they ask people to donate money to buy 114-litre amounts of jet fuel. After an appeal on the Internet and publicity in newspapers, money began to pour in. The team soon had what they needed. They were set to go for the record.

**Slow start**
The first land speed record was set in 1898 by Gaston de Chasseloup-Laubat. His final speed was 63 kph. Today, a bicycle racer could beat this!

**Old record**
The previous land speed record holder, *Thrust 2*, took the record in 1983 at 1,018 kph.

**A speedy truck?**
*Endeavor* holds the truck land speed record. *Thrust SSC* is still more than three times faster!

**A speedy car?**
The *Maclaren F1*, the fastest street-legal car in the world, can reach 370 kph. That's less than a third as fast as the *SSC*.

October 15, 1997 was a perfect autumn day. It was perfect weather too for trying to set a new speed record. As Andy Green, driver of the SSC, eased open the throttle, the giant black car began to roll. It moved slowly at first so its jets didn't inhale desert dust. As it picked up speed, the afterburners began to blaze and poke their 12-metre-long tongues of flame out behind the engines. It was an amazing sight.

The driver sat so low he could only see 3 km ahead. To keep on course he followed a white line of gypsum powder the team had sprinkled on the desert floor.

Halfway along the track was a measured 1.6 km. By the time the car got there it was travelling at 1,228 kph. That's slightly faster than the speed of sound. It zipped through 1.6 km in under five seconds.

Onlookers saw the 10-tonne jet car slip past as steady as a locomotive on rails, chased by a 90-metre-wide carpet of desert dust lifted by the trailing shock wave. A few seconds later the double crack of *Thrust*'s two jet engines breaking the sound barrier split the air.

Two minutes after it set off, the car came to a stop. It was 20 km from where it started. *Thrust SSC* was the proud owner of a new world record.

**A speedy plane?**
A *747* crew, flying overhead at the right moment, would have been shocked to see *Thrust SSC* moving 290 kph faster than it was flying.

**Catching up**
*Thrust SSC* broke the sound barrier on the ground exactly 50 years after the first plane, the *X-1*, did so in the air.

**What about people?**
The fastest person in the world can run 100 metres in just under 10 seconds. That's about 38 kph.

## Think tiny
Enlarged here, the world's tiniest car is the size of a match head. It is a working model of a 1936 Toyota – but it's 1,000 times smaller.

## Think bigger
One of the smallest cars you may spot is the Smart from Daimler Benz. Two will fit into a normal-sized parking space.

# Stretch limousine

The first thing the lottery winner did with his prize was to buy the best Cadillac he could. Then he told friends he was going to cut it in half. He wanted a stretch limousine – and that is how they are made!

The car was sent to a special limo-building factory. The owner asked for a "120-inch super stretch limo." That meant the factory would open the car up and lengthen the body by 120 inches, or three metres.

The cutters sliced the car as easily as a knife cuts into butter. In went long steel rails and new side panels. Then the car's interior was designed.

A partition divided the chauffeur and passenger compartments. It had an electric window that slid up and down. Big, soft leather seats were also fitted. Ten people could now sit in the car. With a refrigerator, a telephone, a TV and a video, the finished interior looked nothing like a normal car.

With a short stretch of the imagination, it reminded the owner of a luxurious yacht. But instead of a hull it had wheels!

**All jazzed up**
Limousines are usually luxuriously fitted inside. Neon lights and painted ceilings add to the glamour.

**How long?**
You could park six large family cars alongside the world's longest stretch limousine.

19

# Deep-sea submersible

Two scientists and a pilot climbed down into *Alvin*, a deep-sea submersible. The hatches clanged shut. Then a crane lifted the little craft over the ship's side and gently set it down on the waves.

**Getting dark**
There is no light 900 metres below sea level. Submersibles depend on powerful lights if they are going deeper.

*Once in the water,* Alvin *is stable enough for a person to stand on its top.*

**Going down**
Scuba divers can dive to 50 metres before the pressure stops them. In an atmospheric diving suit, a diver can go to ten times that depth.

The 7-metre-long diving vessel bobbed on the swell and then dipped underwater. Now it moved more like a spaceship than a sea-going ship as it gracefully began to sink.

Its journey would take it down almost 4 km into the inky black ocean depths. The descent would take just over two hours.

*Alvin*'s crew was glad to be wearing thermal underwear and heavy jumpers. The water outside was icy cold and that affected the temperature inside. As they huddled in the tiny cabin, only one light was kept on to save power. It was eerily quiet, though the crew did keep in regular contact with the ship above through a cordless telephone.

As it neared the sea floor, *Alvin* halted and the pilot flipped on a bank of powerful lights. The crew peered out of *Alvin*'s portholes. What would they see?

**Going deeper**
In the deepest parts of the sea, water pressure is 1,000 times greater than at the surface. Normal submarines cannot go this deep – the pressure would flatten them.

**Deeper still**
In 1966, a submersible called the *Trieste* set a world record by diving to more than 11,000 metres.

**Staying down**
*Alvin* can stay under water up to 72 hours in an emergency.

**Deep thoughts**
*Alvin* can dive deeper than a whale. *Trieste* goes deeper still.

Skyscrapers of black rock loomed out of the dark. Nearby were the smoking hot-water vents the scientists had come to study. Heated by volcanic rocks deep in the earth, water gushed out of the vents at temperatures hot enough to melt lead. Yet small plants and animals lived around the vents. The scientists hoped to learn more about their lives.

The pilot brought *Alvin* closer. The machine's big robotic claw swung down to collect samples of the gushing water. The scientists knew this would stink like rotten eggs. Then *Alvin* moved away to settle on the seabed where the scientists could gather further samples.

After four hours, the work was complete. The pilot released metal pellets from a tank to lighten *Alvin*'s load and the craft began the long two-hour journey back to the surface. It had been a fascinating trip.

**What's that?**
This odd-looking racing machine is a swamp buggy. It is raced through muddy swamps in Florida. Swamp buggies were originally built as hunting machines.

# Offshore powerboats

Each year from June to November, powerboat crews from all over Europe and the Middle East gather for a season of races. In open seas they battle to win the World Championships of offshore powerboat racing.

Offshore powerboats are huge. They weigh the same as five family cars and stretch a good 13 metres. Their massive twin hulls, called catamarans, are made out of two space-age materials – carbon fibre and Kevlar.

The combination is lighter than steel but a lot tougher. Into the hulls go two fighter-plane cockpits – one for the driver and one for the throttleman.

The two crew members are strapped into their seats for safety. Both wear life jackets and crash helmets and each has an air supply. They talk to each other, and to team members on shore, through intercoms in their helmets.

The intercoms are vital pieces of equipment. Once a race begins, the roar of the engines means the crew cannot hear each other without them.

**Skirted boats**
Tiny hovercraft race at 135 kph every year at World Championships in France. They follow a water-and-wet-grass circuit.

**One or two?**
Offshore powerboats used to have single hulls and open cockpits. Today's twin-hulled boats, with their closed canopies, are much safer.

**Thin and fast**
Cigarette boats
have won more
races than any
other boats.
They have twin
500-horsepower
engines. They
were originally
used to smuggle
cigarettes
between the
Bahamas
and Florida.

Boats jostle for position when a race begins, narrowly avoiding hitting each other. The race course is marked with anchored floats called buoys. The boats have to manoeuvre round them.

Inside each boat the driver begins checking the navigation system and compass to stay on course. The throttleman watches the wind and waves, trying to guess what the boat will do next.

Running into the wind can speed a boat up, as it lifts the hull out of the water. However, if the boat rises off the top of a wave to fly through the air, the throttle is hauled back. This stops the propeller from spinning too fast and breaking!

The throttleman's constant adjustments can mean the extra kilometre per hour that will win the race. But at speeds of 240 kph, his moves have to be instant!

**Slow down!**
Choppy seas can slow a powerboat by 80 kph or more.

**Jet boats**
In New Zealand, small jet boats are raced up shallow rivers. They have no propeller to catch on the river bed.

**Formula 1 boats**
These racing boats are fast and furious. They seat one person, and, like offshore powerboats, are twin-hulled. They can accelerate from 0 to 160 kph in five seconds.

# Hydroplane racing

Hydroplane racing is the fastest and most dangerous of all watersports. On a 4 km course, the best machines shoot down the straight stretches at 320 kph and take corners at 250 kph. It's thrilling to watch these boats in action.

The hulls barely touch the water. Hydroplanes basically travel on a cushion of air. But the boats shake violently, pounding over the surface of the water like hammers.

The violent motion can temporarily blur the driver's eyesight! Yet over a 20-minute race, drivers must tweak the controls to keep their boat as high out of the water as possible. At the same time they try to overtake other hydroplanes. That's not as easy as it sounds.

A boat that overtakes must not cut in front of the other boat until it is more than five boat-lengths ahead. That's because each boat creates a huge "rooster"-tail of spray that flings a tonne of water into the air. If this pelted down in the path of a following boat, it would flood the cushion of air the boat was riding on. When this happens, it forces the following boat up and over in a spectacular somersault.

**Power crazy**
A hydroplane is ridiculously powerful. Its engine is actually four times more powerful than a Formula 1 car engine.

**No protection**
Hydroplanes used to have open cockpits. But increasing speeds led to more accidents and today's drivers sit in sealed cockpits.

**A way out**
Hydroplanes are fitted with two escape hatches. One is in the front, and one is underneath the boat, located in the hull.

**Speed king**
Hydroplanes, like drag cars, can race over 400-metre lengths. The *Spirit of Texas* set a 400-metre record of 5.5 seconds.

A hydroplane is cleverly designed, with a double front hull but a single rear hull. As it picks up speed its two front hulls become airborne. This means it doesn't have a huge weight of water to move aside. With only the back hull and propeller dragging in the water, most of its power turns straight into speed.

The secret of hydroplane racing, though, is what the boats use to push themselves along with. They are fitted with a giant helicopter engine.

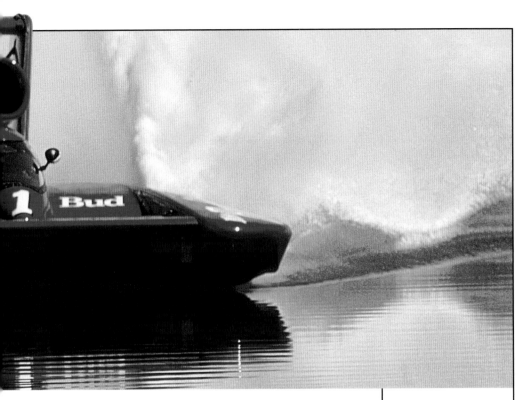

The engine is fine-tuned to produce an incredible 4,200 horsepower. That's enough power to run 42 good-sized family cars!

The engine does its job, but the speed puts lives in danger. In the past, hydroplaning has killed many drivers. That's why today's drivers sit cocooned in a sealed cockpit fitted with escape hatches and an oxygen supply. Accidents still happen with these speed monsters, but nowadays drivers usually survive.

**Strange brew**
Many hydroplane engines run on alcohol, gas, or other strange brews of fuel. These give more power than the petrol or diesel we use for cars.

**Next in line**
After the
*Mi-26*, the
next biggest
helicopter is the
*Chinook.*
Its freight hold
is a third as big
as the Mi-26's.

**Smallest of all**
There's only
room for one
in the world's
smallest
helicopter.
In fact it only
weighs as much
as a small adult.

# *Mi-26* helicopter

The twin engines coughed and belched smoke as one of the world's largest helicopters, Russia's *Mi-26*, started up. The noise was tremendous.

Moments later, the helicopter's eight rotor blades began to whisk the air, stirring up the dust beneath. They gathered speed and merged into a whirring disc that was wide enough to park ten lanes of cars beneath it.

At last, with a great clatter, the mammoth helicopter shrugged once and heaved itself into the air. It was on an emergency mission in the Ural Mountains of Russia, where a series of forest fires raged. The fires had already charred huge areas of forest. They were now nearing roads and villages.

The five-man crew of the *Mi-26*
had scrambled into the air minutes
after the call came through.
Their job was to ferry firefighters
to the scene of the blaze.

**Power pack**
The *Mi-26*'s
twin engines
are 60 times as
powerful as a
truck's engine.

АЭРОФЛОТ

That's why 78 firefighters were
now crammed together on the
helicopter's cargo deck. Each was
fitted out with a parachute and a
large pack of firefighting equipment.
They were ready for the drop and the
task ahead of them.

**Tanked up**
The *Mi-26*'s
fuel tanks could
power a family
car halfway
round the
world. They
can take the
*Mi-26* 480 km.

**60 years ago**
In 1939,
a Russian
engineer named
Sikorsky, living
in the U.S.A.,
built the first
working single-
rotor helicopter.

**1,500 years ago**
The idea
behind a
helicopter is
more than
1,500 years old.
Back then, the
Chinese had a
toy called a
flying top that
used feathered
rotors to fly.

**Back and forth**
A helicopter's
rotor blades tilt
in two directions
so a helicopter
can fly forwards
and backwards.

As they reached the fires, the helicopter crew could see a wall of smoke. They could not see through it, but several kilometres west of the smoke line the pilot spotted a winding logging road. This was their drop zone. The tree-lined road was too narrow to set the *Mi-26* down, so the pilot hovered at about 450 metres while the crew lowered the cargo deck's rear hatch.

In waves, the firefighters dived head-long out of the helicopter. Parachutes snapped open and they drifted down onto the road. Ten minutes later, all 78 men were safely on the ground and the crew were raising the hatch.

The giant helicopter dipped its nose and headed back to base to collect more firefighters.

АЗРОФЛОТ

3141

# The *X-15*

The giant *B-52* bomber rumbled down the runway and lifted off. It carried no bombs. Instead a small black dart was tucked under its right wing like a rolled-up newspaper.

The dart was an X-15, a U.S. Air Force experiment to see if it was possible to fly an occupied plane into space. By hitching a ride on the B-52, the X-15 halved the fuel it needed to get airborne. It carried one pilot and was basically a flying fuel tank. It had stubby wings on its sides and a rocket engine on its back.

The *X-15* was the fifteenth in a line of experimental aircraft that began with the *X-1*.

The original goal of
these planes was to go
higher than 30 km and faster than
three times the speed of sound.
The *X-15* achieved this, and more.
It was the first plane ever to fly into
space. And it broke all records for
being the highest, fastest and most
dangerous way to fly.

Suddenly the *X-15* left the *B-52*.
Its engine fired and it climbed
straight up as if aiming to punch
a hole in the sky. By the time it
reached 60 km there was so little
air left that its wings
had nothing to bite
into anymore.

*X-1*
The *X-1* was
the first plane
to fly faster
than the speed
of sound.

**Wrong engine**
If the *X-15* had
been fitted with
a jet engine, it
would have
spluttered and
died long before
reaching space.
A jet engine
needs air, and
there is no air
in space.

*The* X-15
*had skids
instead of
rear wheels.*

The *X-15* now used a dozen tiny rockets to steer itself. Up and up it climbed. By the time it was out of fuel it was more than 100 km up. The pilot could see the curve of the planet and look down on the atmosphere he had left behind.

There is no clear line where atmosphere ends and space begins. Most people in space exploration agree that it happens at about 80 km up. That's why this pilot, and half his colleagues, earned themselves the right to wear astronaut wings. For at the top of its flight the *X-15* was travelling like a spaceship.

**Low fliers**
High-flying passenger jets cruise around the world at a height of about 12 km. Compared to this the *X-15* went nine times higher.

66672

U.S. AIR F

FUEL VENT

USAF

By now the *X-15* was rocketing along at about 7,200 kph. That's just over six times the speed of sound. At normal motorway speeds, a car would have to travel non-stop for three days and nights to go as far as the *X-15* would have done had it kept this up for an hour.

Turning back to Earth, the plane glided down. It was a strange sight. To save weight, it had no rear wheels, only a pair of metal skids – a bit like gigantic skis. After landing, it simply skied along the ground until it stopped. The flight had taken just over ten minutes.

**Hot stuff**
At six times the speed of sound, the *X-15*'s skin got very hot, reaching a scorching 650°C. It had a special metal surface to withstand this.

**Getting bigger**
Even slower planes, such as Concorde, heat up in supersonic flight. Heat makes metal expand. Concorde's body swells 20 cm in flight.

**Earlier trips**
Before the space shuttle, astronauts were sent into space in rockets. The giant *Saturn V* rockets were the largest and the most powerful launchers built.

*Saturn V*

**Speed record**
In orbit the shuttle flies 30 times faster than a jumbo jet. It would take ten minutes to fly from Los Angeles to New York.

# Space shuttle

The Crawler inched towards the launch pad. At its fastest, the world's largest transport machine could almost get up to walking speed. Now it was travelling at half that pace because of the load on its deck.

The load was the space shuttle, the only plane that can ferry astronauts to and from space under its own power.

USA  United States  NASA  Atlantis

The shuttle consists of an orbiter, which carries a crew of seven astronauts, a giant fuel tank and two skinny booster rockets. On this trip, the orbiter also carried a satellite to launch in space.

Six hours later, countdown reached zero. With a roar and a blinding glare, the shuttle shot up. Two minutes later, the now empty booster rockets broke free.
The main engines thundered on, draining the fuel tank at a speed that would empty a swimming pool in under ten seconds. The emptied fuel tank soon dropped away and the orbiter glided gently into its path around Earth. The seven astronauts were 300 km up.

**Empties**
When empty, the two booster rockets drop back to Earth. They are collected to be used again.

The shuttle's robotic arm is as long as four cars parked bumper to bumper.

In space the astronauts and their equipment became weightless. It was fun, but they had a lot of work to do if they were to launch the satellite.

**Space chair**
Astronauts use a rocket-propelled "armchair" when they work outside the shuttle.

Two astronauts climbed into their spacesuits and entered the orbiter's whale-sized cargo bay. The enormous cargo bay doors swung open. The astronauts then used a long robotic arm to begin the process of launching the satellite.

Checking and launching the satellite took seven days.

Then it was time to return to Earth. Strapped back into their seats, the astronauts heard the puff of the steering rockets. Then the main engine fired. Its power would take the craft out of orbit and turn it to Earth.

When the orbiter hit Earth's atmosphere it started to buck and plunge. Meanwhile, the craft blazed red with the heat of dropping through the air at thousands of kilometres an hour. Special ceramic tiles stopped it from melting.

The orbiter no longer needed its engines. It returned to Earth as a glider, making a neat runway landing.

**Space station**
Countries with space programmes are planning a jointly run space station in Earth's orbit. Its permanent crew will show that humans can live in space.

**Life on board**
In space, the orbiter's seven crew members live in a section at the front of the shuttle. The rest of the craft is a cargo bay – and the massive engines.

# Ideas for the future

Ideas for machines of the future may sound odd. But imagine how weird a space shuttle would have seemed to people one hundred years ago.

The Cadillac *Evoq* is a luxury sports car of the future. If you are ever offered a ride in one, don't reach for the door handles. There are none – the car opens by remote control!

The car can also "see" in the dark. A camera picks up the body heat of people and animals well beyond the beam of the headlights. Their image appears on the windscreen, warning drivers to steer clear.

**No fuel tank!**
People who make new machines try to find ways to save power. This solar-powered car runs on energy from the Sun.

**Speak to me**
The *Evoq* has an on-board, voice-controlled computer. It helps the driver to travel safely.

The car can detect anything behind it in the same way. The *Evoq* is a smart car.

On water, the little *Flarecraft L-325* is a boat dressed up like a plane. Known as a wingship, it has a pair of stubby wings, an aeroplane's tail, and a small propeller above the roof.

As the 9-metre-long craft speeds up, its wings create a cushion of high-pressure air on the water's surface. The cushion is strong enough to lift the five-passenger wingship into the air, where it speeds along at 120 kph. It's much faster than a boat because the water isn't dragging it back. Yet it can't rise up more than the height of an adult.

That's why the wingship will never be anything but a "boat." The moment it tries to fly higher, the air cushion vanishes and the craft splashes down.

**Water flight**
As the *Flarecraft®* speeds up, it rises in the water. At 80 kph, it takes off and cruises just above the water's surface.

**What's that?**
This design for a car shows how unusual some ideas for new machines can look. It's called the *Slug.*

**Speed monsters**
Supersonic
planes of the
future will be
more than
twice as long
as Concorde!

**Space rescue**
This is a
suggested
rescue craft for
ferrying people
back from an
international
space station if
it should ever
be needed.

There are exciting plans for
future air travel as well. Designers
are hard at work on a 300-seat jet
aeroplane that flies at 2,400 kph.
That's over twice the speed of sound!
The plane will travel from the U.S.
to Japan in four hours. Right now
the trip between the two countries
takes more than twice as long!

As the plane will travel faster
than a bullet, its nose and wing
edges will heat to temperatures hot
enough to bake a cake. That's a
problem for a plane. It will have
to be made of metals that can
take repeated heating and
cooling without weakening. If a
metal weakens, it can fracture.

There's another problem. An aeroplane that breaks the speed of sound, or a supersonic aeroplane, has to have a long, pointed nose. But it's difficult for pilots to see past the nose when they land and take off. Concorde solves this problem with a nose that lifts and droops, but it's heavy. The new plane will have no front windows! Instead there will be a big display in the cockpit, showing what's ahead.

The possibilities for machines of the future are fascinating. Here is one unusual design for a futuristic space transporter. What do *you* think extreme machines will look like?

# Glossary

**Aerodynamic**
The smooth, stream-lined shape that helps a car or aeroplane to slip through air easily.

**Circuit**
A set course round which machines can race.

**Drag racer**
The name given to cars and motorbikes which race short distances (usually 400 metres) in a straight line.

**Endurance race**
A race run over a long distance which takes a long time. Driving skill and a reliable engine are more important than speed.

**Fuel**
The material that powers an engine to make it go.

**Gears**
These control the speed of an engine.

**Glider**
Any aeroplane that doesn't have an engine to drive it is a glider. When the space shuttle runs out of fuel to power its engine, it becomes a glider. It glides back down to Earth.

**Grandstand**
A seating area for a crowd watching a sporting event.

**Horsepower**
A means of measuring an engine's power.

**Hull**
The part of a boat that sits in the water.

**Hydroplane**
A fast motorboat that skims over the water with most of its hull in the air. At speed, the flat shape of the hull planes across the surface, rather than cutting through the water. Hydroplanes are the fastest racing boats.

**Jet engine**
All engines run on two things: fuel and oxygen. Jet engines gulp their oxygen from air.

**Land speed record**
The fastest speed set by a vehicle on land. The record has been broken many times. It is now faster than the speed of sound.

**Rocket engine**
A rocket engine carries the oxygen it needs in a tank in a special substance called an oxidiser. See also **Jet engine**.

**Rotors**
The whirling blades above a helicopter are known as rotors because of the way they spin. Each rotor is a mini-wing that lifts as it rotates.

**Shock wave**
Anything going faster than the speed of sound creates a shock wave in the air. We hear it as a loud bang. It can shatter glass at close range. If you could see it, it would look a bit like the front, or bow, wave that big, fast-moving ships create.

**Space shuttle**
The space shuttle is made up of an orbiter, two booster rockets and a fuel tank. The orbiter can return to space again and again.

**Speed of sound**
Sound moves very much slower than light – that's why you see lightning before you hear it. At ground level, where air is thickest, sound travels at about 1,224 kph.

**Submersible**
A submarine cruises underwater as well as diving and climbing. A submersible mainly just dives and climbs. Submersibles are carried to a new site by a mother ship and then lowered over the side.

**Throttle**
The control handle or pedal that feeds fuel to an engine. As it is opened, more fuel is pumped in and the engine speeds up. To slow down, the throttle has to be closed.